263 BRAIN BUSTERS

263

BRAIN BUSTERS

Just How Smart Are You, Anyway?

BY LOUIS PHILLIPS

Illustrated by James Stevenson

Puffin Books

PUFFIN BOOKS
Published by the Penguin Group
A division of Penguin Books USA Inc.,
375 Hudson Street, New York, New York 10014, U.S.A.
Penguin Books Ltd, 27 Wrights Lane, London W8 5TZ, England
Penguin Books Australia Ltd, Ringwood, Victoria, Australia
Penguin Books Canada Ltd, 10 Alcorn Avenue, Toronto, Ontario, Canada M4V 3B2
Penguin Books (N.Z.) Ltd, 182-190 Wairau Road, Auckland 10, New Zealand

Penguin Books Ltd, Registered Offices: Harmondsworth, Middlesex, England

First published in 1985 in simultaneous hardcover and paperback
editions by Viking Kestrel and Puffin Books.
12 14 16 18 20 19 17 15 13

Printed in the United States of America by
R. R. Donnelley & Sons Company, Harrisonburg, Virginia
Set in Aster.

Library of Congress Cataloging-in-Publication Data
Phillips, Louis. 263 brain busters.
Summary: A collection of mathematical and verbal brain-teasing questions interspersed with
"brain vacation" jokes.
1. Puzzles—Juvenile literature. 2. Mathematical recreations—Juvenile literature. 3. Literary
recreations—Juvenile literature. [1. Puzzles. 2. Mathematical recreations. 3. Literary rec-
reations] I. Stevenson, James, ill. II. Title. III. Title: Two hundred sixty-three brain
busters.
GV1493.P558 1985b   793.73   85-40446   ISBN 0 14 03.1875 5

For
Ivan, Delia, Eric & Kai Johnson
L. P.

CONTENTS

CHAPTER ONE

...

If King Midas
Sits on Gold,
Who Sits on Silver?

OR

*30 Questions to Put Your Brain
into High Gear*

1 It is a dark and freezing night, and you have been wandering about in a blizzard for three hours. You finally spy a log cabin, and you (with a great deal of difficulty) finally reach the cabin's door. Inside the cabin you discover a wood-burning stove, a kerosene lamp, an oil burner, and one candle. You reach into your coat pocket and discover that you have only one match. You study the objects in the room carefully. What will you light first?

2 Two women lived in a small cabin by the lake. They were both expert runners, and they both ran exactly at the same speed. However, when the first woman ran around the lake she covered the distance in one hour and 20 minutes; when the second woman ran around the lake in the opposite direction of the first woman, she covered the distance in only 80 minutes. How is that possible?

3 Nikki went to bed at 9 P.M., and she set her alarm clock so that she would wake up the next morning at

10:00. How many hours of sleep would Nikki get before the alarm clock woke her?

4 Leslie and Lorna have the same parents. Leslie and Lorna look exactly alike. Leslie and Lorna are the same age, yet they are not twins. How is this possible?

5 John was born on December 28th, yet his birthday always comes in the summer. How can this be?

6 Imagine a ship in the middle of the ocean. The ship has a rope ladder that hangs over the side so that its bottom rung just touches the top of the water. Each rung of the ladder is five inches away from the rung above it and from the rung below it. How many rungs will be under water when the tide has risen five feet?

7 What planet has canals, ice caps, and an atmosphere?

8   What question can a person ask all day long, always get completely different answers, and yet all the answers could be correct?

9   Why didn't the United States Government, in 1800, bury Benedict Arnold with full military honors?

10   Louis is carrying a sack of potatoes, Jim, however, is able to carry three sacks of the very same size. Louis's load is still heavier than Jim's. Why?

11   What is certain to go out the tighter it is locked in?

12   Two mothers and two daughters went to the store, and each bought a brand-new bicycle. Yet only three bicycles were sold to them. How is this possible?

13 A man was once married to the sister of his widow. How could that be?

14 When the day after tomorrow is yesterday, to-day will be as far from Tuesday as today was from Tuesday when the day before yesterday was tomorrow. What day is it?

15 Two chess players got up one Monday and played six games of chess. The first player won four games and lost two. His roommate also won four games and lost two. How is that possible?

16 If Peter Piper picked a peck of pickled peppers, how many pickled peppers did Peter Piper pick?

17 In a certain city, 5% of all the persons in town have unlisted phone numbers. If you select 100 names at random from that city's phone directory, how many people selected will have unlisted phone numbers?

18 There is a horse tied to a rope. The rope is 10 feet long. There is a bale of hay 23 feet in front of the horse. The horse is able to eat the hay, yet does not break the rope. How is that possible?

19   There are three houses—a blue house, a red house, and a white house. The red house is to the right of the house in the middle; the blue house is to the left of the house in the middle. Now where is the white house?

20   An electric train is traveling west. There is an 18 mph wind blowing from the north. Which way will the smoke blow?

21   Not long ago a man went on a hunting trip. Soon he was down to his final bullet. He came on a panther, puma, and mountain lion. He squeezed the trigger and, using only one bullet, he killed them all. How is that possible?

22   You have a glass filled to the top. You hold it straight out in front of you and you let it fall to the floor. Is it possible for the glass to fall without spilling any water?

23 On the current one-cent postage stamp, does George Washington face right or left?

24 Which is better—an old one hundred-dollar bill or a new one?

25 A baseball game was held, and the final score was 1–0, yet not a single man crossed home plate. How was that possible?

26 After a man had been blindfolded, someone hung up his hat. The man walked 100 yards, turned around, and shot a bullet through his hat. How is such a feat possible?

27 A man placed his pen on top of a table. When he got up in the morning, the pen was gone. No one had taken the pen, but the pen was recovered three miles down the road. How could that be?

28   Can you name at least three things that are filled when they are used, but empty when they are not in use?

29   Can you name at least three objects that are more useful upside down than they are right side up?

30   What is cured only after it's dead?

31   At a posh restaurant I was having dinner with a noted historian. We were discussing the relative merits of the life of Woodrow Wilson, when my friend turned to me and said, "I'll tell you all you need to know about the character of Woodrow Wilson. Why, when he ran for President, his own mother didn't even vote for him!"

"Is that true?" I asked.

"Of course, it's true," he said. "I know whereof I speak."

That ended the discussion. I didn't realize until I arrived home that, although my friend spoke the truth, I had been tricked. How had I been misled?

32   All right—you knew we'd ask this one: If King Midas sits on gold, who sits on silver?

CHAPTER TWO

Let's Jog Your Memory, or a Quick Sprint Through Classic Problems

• • •

33 A woman goes into a pet store to purchase a mynah bird. The man selling the bird tells the woman, "I guarantee that this bird will repeat every word it hears." Ten days later the woman takes the mynah bird back to the pet shop.

"I want my money back," the woman complains. "You lied to me. This bird doesn't speak at all."

"Ah, but I didn't lie to you, madam," the salesman tells her. And the salesman was indeed telling her the truth, the whole truth, and nothing but the truth. How is that possible?

34 If three cats catch three mice in three minutes, how many cats will you need to catch 100 mice in 100 minutes?

35 A brave explorer was once exploring deepest, darkest Africa when he was captured by a tribe of cannibals. The cannibals, however, were fond of problems in logic, and so they said to the explorer,

"We are going to allow you to make one statement. If the statement you make is true, we will burn you alive at the stake. If the statement you make is false, then we will boil you alive in a huge pot of water."

The explorer, however, was very clever, for he had read this book. He made a statement, and the logic-loving cannibals were forced to let him go. What statement did he make?

36 A millionaire hired a butler who was blind. He said to the butler, "In my room there is a bureau. Inside the top drawer of the bureau I have seventy-five pairs of white socks and seventy-five pairs of black socks. I want to wear a matching pair of socks, but I don't care if they're black or white."

"Very good, sir," the butler replied.

What is the least number of socks that the butler can bring back to make certain that his master has a pair of the same color?

37 There was a farmer who owned a goose, a fox, and a bag of corn. He had to carry the goose, the fox, and the bag of corn to an island, but his rowboat was so tiny that he could fit only himself and one other item or animal in it. How was he able to transfer the goose, the fox, and the bag of corn from the farm to the island without leaving the fox and the goose together (if he did that, the fox would surely eat the goose) or the goose alone with the bag of corn (if he did that, the goose would surely eat the corn)?

38 There is a well that is 25 feet deep. At the bottom of the well there was a frog. To get out of the

well, the frog would make one leap a day. He would leap up three feet and then he would fall back two feet. How many days did it take him to get out of the well?

39 A man, buying steaks for his restaurant, approached a butcher. "How many steaks do you have for sale?" the restaurant owner asked. "I have twenty-five steaks for sale," the butcher answered. "And how much are they?" "The steaks cost six dollars apiece if I pick them out," the butcher said, "and eight dollars apiece if you pick them out."

How did the buyer get the best deal for his money?

40 A man is placed in a prison cell. There is only one window—a small skylight directly overhead. The skylight is 12 feet from the floor. The walls are made of reinforced concrete, and the walls extend four feet underground. The floor is a dirt floor. Although the prisoner has no hope of tunneling his way to freedom, he starts to dig a tunnel. Why?

41   A man carrying three croquet balls comes to a swinging bridge. The bridge is not very sturdy. A sign by the bridge states that it cannot hold more than 175 pounds. The man weighs 171 pounds, and each of the croquet balls weighs two pounds. The man merely shrugs and carries the three croquet balls across the bridge. Why doesn't the bridge collapse?

42   A friend comes to you and says, "I have hidden a hundred-dollar bill in one of the books in my library. The hundred-dollar bill is located between pages 75 and 76 of the book. If you can locate the book, you may keep the money." Would you look for the $100 bill?

43   There are two volumes of a dictionary standing side by side on a library shelf. Each volume is two inches thick, with each of its covers one-eighth of an inch thick. A bookworm starts crawling, in a straight line, from the first page of Volume I to the last page of Volume II. How far will the bookworm travel?

44   The rhyme below is quite old, but it is still quite tricky. Can you figure it out?

> *Ten fish I caught without an eye,*
> *And nine without a tail;*
> *Six had no head, and half of eight*
> *I weighed upon the scale.*
> *Now who can tell me as I ask it,*
> *How many fish were in my basket?*

45   Can you prove that no one in America spends any time working?

BRAIN VACATION No. 1.
Now that you've solved the hard questions, try your
mind on these fun questions!

46 A man and a woman were eating dinner in a
fancy restaurant. When the waiter appeared, the
woman ordered steak and a baked potato. The man
ordered lobster, champagne, and dessert. When the
waiter entered the kitchen, he told the cook that the
lobster was for an admiral. How did the waiter know
that the man who placed the order was an admiral?

47 A person goes to a post office to mail a letter. She
purchases two stamps and then asks the next person
standing in line to put the stamps on the envelope
for her. Now why didn't she put the stamps on herself?

48 If bananas come under the heading of fruit, and
radishes come under vegetables, what do eggs come
under?

49   How is it possible to shave three times a day and still grow a beard?

50   There are 10 sheep walking in a straight line across a field. Which sheep can look back and say, "I am the third from the last in line"?

51   Why is it very rare for the temperature in Florida to change rapidly?

CHAPTER THREE

Verbal Gymnastics, or a Word to the Wise and a Few Words for You, Too!

...

52 Using the letters *C* and *Y*, can you spell a five-letter word that is good to eat?

53 What word of one syllable becomes a two-syllable word when you take two letters away?

54 Can you rearrange the letters of the phrase "best in prayer" to get the name of a religious group?

55 Can you think of any words in the English language that do not contain vowels?

56 Here's a project for a rainy day. Take out a good dictionary, turn to the entries listed under the letter *I*, and see if you can locate a *14*-letter word that repeats the same vowel six times.

57 There are five words in the English language that end in *cion*. Can you think of one such word?

58 For this problem you want to come up with a six-letter word. When you reverse the third and fourth letters of that word, the new word formed means the exact opposite of the original word. What is the word? (Hint: The word you are seeking begins with *U*.)

59 From which word of five letters can you take away two letters and have one remaining?

60 What word is it that, if you take the whole away, some remains?

61 Can you take three letters away from a four-letter word and yet not change its meaning?

62 How do you spell Boston backwards?

63 Can you name an eight-letter word that contains *KST* in the middle, in the beginning, and at the end?

64 Can you decipher what the following symbol represents: *d O*?

65   Can you decipher the following rebus?

OY UR ill; PIE $\dfrac{\text{LEM}}{\text{ADE}}$ w_{ill} $\begin{smallmatrix}u\\u\end{smallmatrix}$

66   What word can be pronounced quicker by adding a syllable to it?

67   One word on this page is mispelled. Can you locate it?

68   Can you punctuate the following statements correctly so that they make sense? (Hint: You will need to use five periods and a question mark.)

That that is is that that is not is not that that is is not that that is not that that is not is not that that is is that not not it it is

69   What do you notice about the following sentence?
I am too cold there inside Alaskan climates.

70 The letters on the top row of a standard typewriter are:

QWERTYUIOP

Can you make a ten-letter word from the above letters? (Yes, you may repeat letters.)

71 From what word of six letters can you take away
one and still have 12?

72 What is the easiest way to change *first* to *last*?

73 Can you name two words in the English language that remain the same even if you turn them
upside down?

74 The word *persuasion* is just one word in the English language that contains each of the five vowels
(*A,E,I,O,U*) just once. Can you think of five more ex-
amples?

75 What do the following words have in common:

ECHO
COB
COOK
BED
BOX
CHICK ?

76 There is at least one three-letter word in the English language that does not change its meaning if you
rearrange those three letters. Can you figure out the
word?

77   What do the following sentences have in common?

> *The quick brown fox jumps over a lazy dog.*
> *Pack my box with five dozen liquor jugs.*

78   What state of the United States uses only four letters to spell its name of 11 letters?

79   I hope you won't deny this fact, but there is only one word in the English language that ends in *ENY*. What word is it?

80   A nine-letter word in the English language contains only one vowel. Do you know it?

81   Starting with the number *one*, what is the first number that uses the letter *A* when its name is spelled out?

82   Is it true that California begins with a *C* and ends with an *E*?

83   Can you name two kinds of automobiles that start with *T*?

84   What does GHOUGHPHTHEIGHTTEEAU spell?

85   If the plural of goose is geese, what is the plural of mongoose?

86   If the wife of the King is called the Queen, then what is the wife of an Earl called?

87   What do the following words and names have in common:

> Fiji
> Seiji Ozawa
> hijinks
> Nijinsky ?

BRAIN VACATION No. 2.
Now that you've solved the hard questions, try tackling a few more silly ones.

88 Where does Thursday come before Wednesday?

89 O.K. We were just kidding about the previous question and answer. Now let's get serious. Where does Thursday come before Wednesday?

90 What is the third hand on a watch or clock called?

91 What do Paul Jones, Clyde Van Dusen, George Smith, and Omar Khayyam all have in common?

92 A man ventured forth for a walk in the country. He didn't carry an umbrella. He didn't wear a hat, and he didn't take refuge under a shelter of any kind, and yet not one hair on his head got wet. Why? (No, he wasn't bald!)

93 O.K. We were just kidding about the previous question and answer. Let's try it again. A man ventured forth for a walk in the country. It started to rain. He didn't carry an umbrella. He didn't wear a hat, and he didn't take refuge under a shelter of any kind. Still, not one hair on his head got wet. Why?

94 True or false: The great artist Michelangelo painted the Sistine Chapel on his back.

95   When did Christmas and New Year's Day fall in the same year?

96   What kind of stone gets lighter the more you carry it around?

97   Which is lighter—milk or cream?

98   Which is heavier—a pound of steel or a pound of potatoes?

99   How can you drop an uncooked egg three feet without breaking it?

100   A man fell off a 20-foot ladder and landed on the sidewalk, but he did not get hurt. Why not?

101   Would you rather have a bruise on your ankle or seven holes in your head?

102   Is it possible to name the capital of each and every one of the United States in less than 50 seconds?

103   What has eight wheels but can carry only one passenger?

104   What makes more noise when it is dead than when it was alive?

...

CHAPTER FOUR

Boy, Do We Have Your Number Now, or There Is No Accounting for Taste

...

105 Some time ago three men were traveling through the English countryside. They were very tired and very hungry, so they entered an inn and immediately ordered a platter of boiled potatoes for dinner. Before the owner even brought the platter of potatoes, the three men fell asleep. After a while one of the men woke up, saw the platter of potatoes, and decided to help himself to his share. He ate one-third of all the potatoes on the platter and then went back to sleep. The second man awoke and, seeing the platter of potatoes, decided to eat what he thought was his share. He ate one-third of the potatoes on the platter and fell asleep. The third man awoke, saw the platter, and, thinking the other two men hadn't eaten yet, decided to eat only his share—one-third of the potatoes on the platter. When the third man finished eating what he thought was his share, there were eight potatoes left on the dish.

How many potatoes were on the platter at the beginning?

106   Mr. and Mrs. Harris have quite a few children. There are eight daughters in the Harris family. Each daughter has two brothers. How many children are there in the Harris family?

107   Can you arrange four 5's so that they equal 6?

108   A fish weighs 10 pounds plus half of its weight. How much does it weigh?

109   You have exactly 100 coins that total $5. Not one of the coins is a nickel, so what coins do you have?

110   You have two coins that total 15 cents, but one of them is not a dime. How is that possible?

111   Is it possible to have exactly $63 in your pocket in bills, without one of those bills being a dollar bill?

112   Why are 1980 pennies worth almost $20?

113   How many squares are there on a checkerboard?

114   You have a pail that holds four gallons of water and a second pail that holds seven gallons of water. Your father sends you to the well and asks you to bring back five gallons of water. Five gallons exactly. No more. No less. Can you do it?

115   Quick! How much dirt is there in a hole 6 feet long, 8 feet deep, and 10 feet wide?

116   How can five people divide five doughnuts so that everyone gets one doughnut and yet have one doughnut left on the plate?

117   Sarah had a cardboard box that was filled with pears. The box contained 34 pears. She placed the box on the scale and found that the box and the pears weighed 13 pounds. She added 17 more pears to the box and weighed the box and pears again. This time the box weighed 19 pounds.
   What is wrong with this information?

118   Buses leave Boston twice a day heading for Reno, Nevada. Buses leave Reno, Nevada, twice a day heading for Boston. The trip takes five days. If you are traveling to Boston, how many buses will you meet on their way to Reno?

119   The world weighs six sextillion tons. How much more would the earth weigh if all the people in the world built a wall around the earth—a wall eight feet high, three feet wide, out of material that weighs exactly 100 pounds per cubic foot?

120   Can you prove that half of 8 is 3?

121   Can you arrange all the integers from 1 to 9 (including 9) in such a way that the numbers total exactly 100?

122   Can you write down five odd-numbered digits in such a way that they add up to 14?

123   Take five pennies from 100 pennies and what do you have?

124   Which is correct: 18 plus 19 *is* 36. Or 18 plus 19 *are* 36?

125   If a man digs a hole two yards long, two yards wide, and two yards deep in one hour, how long will it take that same man to dig a hole four yards long, four yards wide, and four yards deep, assuming that he digs both holes at the same rate of speed?

126 A pen and a bottle of ink cost $1.10. The pen cost exactly one dollar more than the bottle of ink. What did the pen cost?

127 The object of this puzzle is to find a nine-digit number. The first three numbers equal one-third of the last three. The middle three numbers are the result of subtracting the first three from the last. What is the number? (Hint: The nine-digit number consists of each of the nine integers, 1 through 9, used just once.)

128 Below is a problem in addition. It doesn't look correct, but it is. What is the easiest way to show that the problem below is correct?

$$3\,414$$
$$340$$
$$74813$$
$$\overline{}$$
$$4337483$$

129 How is it possible to subtract 45 from 45 and still get 45 as a total?

130 You have four piles of leaves on your front lawn. You have five piles of leaves in your backyard. When you put the piles together, how many piles of leaves will you have?

131   There are two barrels. Each barrel is 4 feet deep and 2 feet in diameter. One barrel is filled with dimes. The second barrel is filled with quarters. Which barrel should you choose if you want to get the one containing the most money?

132   By inserting two punctuation marks, can you make the following equation correct?

$$560 = 600$$

133   How to make money quickly. Suppose you have a five-dollar bill and you need seven dollars. Here is what you do. You take your five-dollar bill to a pawnshop and you pawn it for four dollars. You then go out and sell your pawn ticket for three dollars. You now have seven dollars. But who has lost on your transaction?

134   You apply for a job and your employer gives you a choice of wages. You can have $25,000 for your month's work, or you can have one penny the first day, two pennies the second day, four pennies the third day, eight pennies the fourth day, and so on—doubling your wages every day until the end of the month of 31 days. Which offer should you accept?

135   Take a pair of dice from one of your games. Shake the dice and toss them on the table. Add the top number and the bottom number of each die. The total for the four faces will be 14. How do I know?

136   Here is a challenge for math fans. Can you arrange the following integers

   1   2   3   4   5   7   8   9

into two groups of four numbers each so that each group adds up to the same sum? It doesn't seem difficult to solve, but can you do it?

137   A man had 35 cows. All but 10 died. How many did he have left?

138   What is the difference between six dozen dozen and half a dozen dozen?

139   Quick. Take out a pencil and a sheet of paper and write down the number eleven thousand, eleven hundred, and two.

140   Below is a simple equation. Can you make it correct (i.e., an equality) by simply adding one straight line? No, you may not cross out the equal sign.

$$11 + 11 + 1 = 1,152$$

141   Using four 9's, can you express the number 100?

142   Divide 80 by one-half and add 15. What is the answer?

143   Can you count quickly from 10 to 5 backwards?

BRAIN VACATION No. 3.

Now that you are a math whiz, the following questions will merely tickle your funny bone:

144   What month has 28 days?

145   A man was playing a game, and he got the highest score of all the persons playing the game. The man, however, got so angry that he vowed never to play the game again. Why?

146   How many seconds are there in a year?

147   Two women are having tea. There is a sugar bowl on the table. In the sugar bowl are nine cubes of sugar. The first woman helps herself to sugar. By the end of the meal all the sugar cubes have been used up, and yet each woman has taken an odd number. How is this possible? No sugar cubes have been broken or divided.

CHAPTER FIVE

...

The Real Stumpers, or If You're So Smart Why Are You Reading This Book?

...

148 What state of the United States has the greatest percentage of its state boundary in shoreline?

149 Here is a question that occurs in Alfred Hitchcock's suspense movie, *The Thirty-nine Steps* (based on an adventure novel by John Buchan): When did Good Friday fall on a Tuesday?

150 A woman arrived in Paris. She searched all over the city for two weeks, but she could not find the Eiffel Tower. Why?

151 Can you name a sport in which the participants do not know the score, the spectators do not know the score, and no one knows the winner until the contest is over?

152 How much silver is there in a ton of German silver?

153 There is one substance in the world that weighs more in its liquid form than it does in its solid form. Can you name it?

154 Is it physically possible for you to stand behind your mother, and for your mother to stand behind you at the same time?

155 The world-famous musician Gioacchino Antonio Rossini composed more than 50 operas before his eleventh birthday. Can you explain how he was able to accomplish such a phenomenal feat?

156 To celebrate her tenth birthday, Anne drove a nail into the trunk of an oak tree. When Anne returned to the tree 15 years later, how much higher was the nail if we assume that the tree grew at the rate of three inches per year?

157   Is it physically possible for two people to stand on a single sheet of paper and still not be able to touch each other—if the paper is a standard page from a newspaper?

158 ˙Quick—how many states in the United States?

159   How many peas are there in a bushel of black-eyed peas?

160   Let's say that you count out a hundred dollars in one-dollar bills in 45 seconds. Counting at that same rate, how long would it take you to count one billion dollars?

161   Sneakers are worn by tennis players. Baseball players wear spikes. Football players wear shoes with cleats. Quick now—in what sport are all-metal shoes worn?

162   How many grooves are there in a 33 ⅓-rpm long-playing record?

163 What animal has four good legs and yet cannot walk on the ground?

164 On September 3, 1752, in America, not one person was born and not one person died. True or false?

165 In what sport do players use rackets but do not use a ball?

166 Where in India was India ink first made—Calcutta or Bombay?

167 True of false: January 1, 2000 A.D., will be the first day of the 21st Century.

168 Can you name three sports in which the winning teams go backwards?

169 How many links in a chain?

170   A man was hired to mow the grass. He took the lawn mower out of the shed and went out. Soon he was back.

He said, "I cannot mow all that grass out there. That grass is a hundred feet high."

He was telling the truth, but how was such a statement possible?

171   True or false: A stack of a billion dollars in one-dollar bills would stand more than 50 miles high.

172   Ten parts of the human body can be spelled with just three letters. Can you name them?

173   Is it possible for anything to be older than its mother?

174   Is it possible for a man to be his own grand-father?

175 How can a pitcher win a baseball game without throwing a single pitch to a batter?

176 In a major-league baseball game a pitcher faced only 27 batters. He retired every batter he faced, allowing no hits and no runs. Still, his team lost the game by the score of 3–0. How is that possible?

177 If a penny is copper-colored, what color is a nickle—silver, copper, or green?

178 Here's a question to try out on people who like Shakespeare. Ask them in what month of the summer does Shakespeare's *A Midsummer Night's Dream* take place.

179 Can you name at least two things that have to be broken before they are used?

180 True or false: Water that has been boiled and allowed to cool will freeze faster than tap water.

181   When you sail from the Atlantic Ocean to the Pacific Ocean by way of the Panama Canal, are you sailing east to west?

182   What do these people have in common: Gail Henley, Mary Calhoun, Sadie Houck, Lena Blackburne, and She Donahue?

183   What is the smallest number that can be written with just three numbers?

184   How many pounds to an ounce? (No, this is not a misprint.)

185   Look carefully at the license plate number written below. Why would it be perfect for someone from Chicago?

$$\mathcal{S}IOUI\ 77I$$

186   What is the easternmost state of the United States?

187   Can you name at least two things that fall but never break? Can you name at least one thing that breaks but never falls?

188   What was the name of the first satellite to go around the earth?

189   Cervantes, Spain's greatest novelist, and William Shakespeare, the great English playwright, both died on April 23, 1616. But they did not die on the same day. Why?

190 What is the fewest number of times a baseball team could come to bat in a nine-inning game?

191 What is the national anthem of Hawaii?

192 The year 1961 was an upside-down one. We mean that you can turn the figure 1961 upside down without changing its value. In the nineteenth century 1881 was an upside-down year. O.K., put on your thinking cap. When will the next upside-down year occur?

193 It is a little-known fact that Harry Davis, in 1896, was the first major-league baseball player to play for two different major-league clubs on the same day. In the opening game of a doubleheader between the New York Giants and the Pittsburgh Pirates, Davis played first base for the Giants. Between games, Davis was traded to the Pirates for first baseman Jake

Beckley. Beckley could have joined Davis in the record books, but he became so angry at the trade that
he refused to play in the second game.

So now the tough question: who played for both
teams in the 1955 World Series?

194 What is the most number of pitches a baseball
player can take in a time at bat in a game without
hitting the ball (i.e., he doesn't hit any fouls) and
without making an out?

195 Why can't a man living in New York City be
buried west of the Mississippi?

196 Who is buried in Grant's tomb?

BRAIN VACATION No. 4.
By now you probably can't be fooled, but we'll keep
trying!

197 You are going on an overnight hiking trip, and
you are facing north. On your right is the east. What
is at your back?

198 The more you take the more you leave behind.
What is it?

199 What can you put inside a barrel to make it
lighter?

200 What do you throw out when you need it and
take in when you don't?

...

CHAPTER SIX

Tricky Questions for Real Wits (and Half-Wits, Too!)

...

201 If you toss it from the top of a high building, it will *not* break, but if you throw it into the ocean, it will break. What is it?

202 What can turn without moving?

203 What goes further the slower it goes?

204 Why is the man who refuses to gamble as bad as a person who does?

205 Do fish bite at sunrise?

206 What building has the most stories?

207 What does a farmer grow if he works day and night?

208 What is the best way to prevent water from coming into your house?

209 What is it that no man wants, but once he has it, he cannot bear to lose it?

210 What grows less tired the more it works?

211 How can you make a slow horse fast?

212 What one thing has done the most to arouse the working class?

213 Can you name something that has to be bad before people consider it to be good?

214 What can be fresh and yet spoiled at the same time?

215 Why would a barber rather shave 10 men from Philadelphia than one from Boston?

216   How can you buy eggs and be certain that there are no chickens in them?

217   What is the best thing to keep in winter?

218   What two documents have contributed the most to the United States Government?

219   What can you see in the water that never gets wet?

220   What goes into the water, under the water, and through the water, but never gets wet?

221   If butter is $1.45 a pound in Chicago, what are windows in Detroit?

222   When you go to the beach for the day, what do you always leave behind?

223   Who weighs more—a six-foot butcher or a five-foot wrestler?

224   What is the best way to raise carrots?

225   What is the easiest thing for a hunter to catch in a heavy winter rain?

226   How many feet in a yard?

227   What is the best way to keep food bills down?

228   What comes before six?

229   What do hippopotamuses have that no other animals have?

230   What animals eat with their tails?

231   What is it that every person, no matter how careful, always overlooks?

232 Do red candles burn longer than yellow ones?

233 In a marathon race what does the winning runner lose?

234 What is neither in the house nor out of the house, but is still part of the house?

235 What eats but never swallows?

236 What is it that we never borrow but often return?

237 What goes on foot but keeps pace with the fastest horse?

238 What gets wetter and wetter the more it dries?

239 What does the richest person in the world make for dinner every night?

240   What pierces your ear without leaving a hole?

241   What kind of person has to be fired before he or she can go to work?

242   What can be only three inches long and three inches wide, yet can contain an entire foot?

243   What is in the Great Wall of China that the Chinese never put there in the first place?

244   What is the best way to make a pair of pants last?

245   What contains more feet in winter than in summer?

246   What divides by uniting and unites by dividing?

247   How many horse tails would it take to reach from New York to San Francisco?

248   Which is faster—heat or cold?

249   What kind of working person drives his customers away?

250   What kind of person finds that his or her business is best when things are dull?

251   If you wear a blue bathing suit in the Red Sea, what happens to it?

252 Two flies are on a table. You swat one. How many are left?

253 What state of the United States is round at both ends and high in the middle?

254 What stays hot even in the refrigerator?

255 Can you name something that you might find in a field, that was never planted in that field, but that you must plow?

256 What is entirely your own but is often used by others, even without your permission?

257 What should you keep after you give it to someone else?

258 What can you hold without touching it?

259 A man in Carson City, Nevada, decides to visit Los Angeles, California. He gets in his car and heads west at the average speed of 55 miles per hour. He drives day and night for four days and yet he does not reach Los Angeles. Why not?

260 Can a man marry three women in a single day (without divorcing any one of them) and yet not break the United States laws?

BRAIN VACATION No. 5.
If you can get past these few wacky questions, you really deserve a month in the country (unless, of course, you are already in the country. In that case, feel free to go somewhere else).

261 What can the citizens of Boston do that no other people can do?

262   What was the color of the dress worn by Queen Elizabeth I at her wedding?

263   Why didn't Beethoven finish The Unfinished Symphony?

CHAPTER SEVEN

...

The Answers!
(Honest!)

...

1   Obviously, you will have to light the match first.

2   They covered equal distance in equal time. One hour and 20 minutes is the same as 80 minutes.

3   If Nikki fell asleep right away, she would get, at the most, one hour of sleep before the alarm clock would go off and wake her.

4   Leslie and Lorna are two members of a set of triplets.

5   John lives in South America. Since the seasons are reversed in the Southern Hemisphere, it is summer there on December 28th.

6   None of the rungs will be under water. As the ship rises, the ladder will rise with it. The bottom rung of the ladder will still reach only the top of the water.

7   Earth. Most people answering this question will say Mars, but there are no canals on Mars.

8   "What time is it now?"

9   The United States Government could not bury Benedict Arnold in 1800, because Benedict Arnold did not die until 1801.

10   The three sacks carried by Jim are empty.

11   A fire is certain to go out the tighter it is locked in, because the supply of oxygen is then cut off.

12   A grandmother, mother, and daughter went to the store.

13   The man married his second wife's sister first.

14   Tuesday.

15   The two chess players did not play chess with each other.

16   None. A person can't pick pickled peppers. Peppers are picked and then the peppers are pickled.

17   None. If their names are in the phone directory, they do not have unlisted numbers.

18   The horse is able to reach the hay because the rope isn't tied to anything.

19   The White House is in Washington, D.C.

20   If the train is run by electricity, there's no smoke.

21   Panther, puma, and mountain lion are all names for one and the same animal.

22   Of course it's possible—if the glass is filled to the top with milk.

23   George Washington does not appear on the current one-cent postage stamp. Benjamin Franklin does.

24   A one-hundred-dollar bill is obviously ninety-nine dollars better than a new *one*.

25   The baseball team consisted of women.

26   His hat was hung over the barrel of the rifle.

27   A pen is a female swan (you might want to check a dictionary on this one). The female swan, or pen, had wandered off on its own.

28   Three things that are filled when they are used, but empty when not in use: Shoe, fountain pen, salt or pepper shaker. (There are other possibilities—a chair, for example.)

29   Some things that are more useful upside down are: a knife (when you are cutting food), a salt or pepper shaker, a phonograph needle, a ketchup bottle.

30   A pig is cured only after it is dead.

31   Of course Woodrow Wilson's mother did not vote for her son. She couldn't. Women didn't have the right to vote before 1920. The first woman, in fact, to cast a vote for her son (Franklin Delano Roosevelt) in a Presidential election was Sara Delano Roosevelt.

32 . The Lone Ranger sits on Silver (his horse).

33   The mynah bird was deaf, so it didn't hear any words at all.

34   The same three cats.

35 The explorer said, "I will be boiled alive in a huge pot of water." When the cannibals heard that statement, they did not know what to do. If the statement were false, they would have to boil him alive, but that would make the statement true, which meant they would have to burn him at the stake, then the statement would have been a false one, which would be that he would have to be boiled alive, and so on. The cannibals had no choice but to allow the explorer to go free.

36 There are only two colors of socks involved—black socks and white ones. To be sure of having a matching pair, all the butler has to do is to bring his master three socks.

37 On the first trip the farmer took the goose across to the island, leaving the fox and the bag of corn at the farm. On the second trip the farmer took the fox to the island, *but he brought the goose back*! On the third trip he took the bag of grain across, leaving the bag of grain on the island with the fox. He then went back and took the goose over to the island.

38   Since the frog leaped forward three feet and fell back two feet, he gained one foot a day. On the twenty-second day, he would be three feet from the top. On his next leap he leaped out of the well and did not fall back. It, therefore, took the frog 23 days to get out of the well.

39   The steak buyer said to the butcher, "I will buy all the steaks and you pick them out."

40   The man in the prison cell piles up the earth until it reaches almost to the skylight, and then he climbs up and breaks the skylight to make his escape.

41   The man carrying the three croquet balls is a juggler. He keeps at least one croquet ball in the air at all times.

42   Don't waste your energy searching for the hundred-dollar bill because your friend is not telling the truth. It's impossible to hide anything between pages 75 and 76 of a book, since they are the front and back of the same page.

43   The bookworm will travel only one-quarter of an inch (one-eighth of an inch + one-eighth of an inch). Why? Because when the two volumes stand in proper order on a bookshelf, the first page of Volume II and the last page of Volume I are separated only by the thickness of the two covers. Look at the books on your own bookshelf and you will see what we mean.

44   The answer is 0, because 10 without the I is 0; 9 without its tail is 0; 6 without its head is 0; half of 8 is 0.

45   Well, let's look at it this way. There are 365 days in a year. Each person sleeps at least eight hours a day, or almost 122 days. That leaves 243 days. Each person, on the average, has eight hours a day of rest. That equals almost another 122 days free from labor. There are now only 121 days for work.

People do not work on Saturdays and Sundays. That accounts for another 104 days of the year. We have only 17 days left in which to do our work. Most people have two weeks of vacation, or 14 days. That leaves only three days. No one works on Christmas Day. That leaves two days. No one works on Memorial Day. Now there is only one day left. That last day is Labor Day, and no one works on that day either! So how does all the work get done?

46   The man was wearing his admiral's uniform.

47   She didn't want the stamps on herself; she wanted the stamps on the envelope.

48   Eggs usually come under hens.

49   If you were a barber, you could shave other men three times a day and still grow your own beard.

50   None. Sheep can't speak.

51 Temperature usually changes by degrees.

52 *C AND Y* spells *candy*!

53 *Plague*. Take the first two letters away, and you have *ague* (pronounced "a'gyoo").

54 *Best in prayer* is an anagram of *Presbyterian*.

55 You can't think of any words without vowels? *Tsk, tsk. Shhh*! I won't rub it in. *Hmm*. . . .

56 One word that fits the requirements is *indivisibility*.

57 Five words in the English language that end in *cion*:

    suspicion
    epinicion
    scion
    coercion
    internecion

You might wish to look up the words in your dictionary to see what they mean.

58 *United*. Its opposite, of course, is *untied*.

59 *Stone*. Take away two letters *(st)*, and you will have *one* left.

60 *Wholesome*.

61 The word is *five*. Take away three letters *(f,i,e,)* and you will have *V* left. *V* is the Roman numeral for five. (We warned you that this is a tricky book!)

62 B-O-S-T-O-N B-A-C-K-W-A-R-D-S.

63   *Inkstand. KST* is in the middle, *IN* is at the beginning, and *AND* is at the end.

64   *d 0* = *decipher* (*D* + zero, which is a cipher).

65   "Boy begone before you are ill; Pie before lemonade will double you up." (The word *boy* has a *b* missing; hence it is begone. *Lem* on *ade* equals lemonade.)

66   *Quick.* Add *er* to it, and it is pronounced *quicker.*

67   *Mispelled* is misspelled on that page. (We hope there aren't any other misspelled words).

68   That that is is. That that is not is not. That that is is not that that is not. That that is not is not that that is. Is that not not it? It is.

69   The first word of the sentence has one letter, the second two letters, the third word has three letters, the fourth word four letters, and so on.

70   Two possible answers are: *typewriter* (yes, *typewriter*—how is that for a coincidence?) and *proprietor.*

71   *Dozens* is a six-letter word. Take away the *S* and you still have a dozen, or twelve.

72   The easiest way to change *first* to *last*: *1st*, add an *a*, and you have *last.*

73   *SWIMS, NOON*—turn them upside down and you still have *SWIMS, NOON.* Other upside-down words: *SIS, dip.*

74   Some possible answers are: *authorize, binoculate, communicable, cautioned, education, equivocal,*

grandiloquent, outspreading.

The words *abstemious* and *facetious* contain the vowels in order.

75 The letters that form those words are symmetrical. If you hold those words upside down in a mirror, the words can be read correctly. Hold other words upside down to a mirror and you will see the difference.

76 One such word is *yea*. You can rearrange the three letters to form *AYE*, which of course means the same thing.

77 Each of those two sentences contains each letter of the alphabet at least once. Can you make up other sentences that use all the letters of the alphabet?

78 *Mississippi* uses only *m, i, s, p.*

79 *Deny.*

80 *Strengths.*

81 The first number that uses *A* in its spelling is *one thousand!*

82 Yes, it's true that *California* begins with a *C*, and that *Ends* begins with an *E*.

83 Automobiles don't start with tea; they start with gasoline.

84   Would you believe POTATO?
     P   sounds like the Gh in *hiccough*.
     O   sounds like the OUGH in *dough*.
     T   sounds like the PHTH in *phthisic*
           (a disease associated with tuberculosis).
     A   sounds like the EIGH in *neighbor*.
     T   sounds like the TTE in *statuette*.
     O   sounds like the EAU in *beau*.
Put them all together and say *potato*!

85   The plural of mongoose is¹ mongooses. Check it
out in the dictionary!

86   The wife of an Earl is a Countess.

87   Each of those four words or names contains three
dotted letters in a row.

88   In the dictionary.

89   Thursday comes before Wednesday at the Inter-
national Date Line. The time zone just east of the In-
ternational Date Line is one whole day earlier than
the zone that lies just west of the line (approxi-
mately 180 degrees longitude). People who travel
eastward pick up one whole day (Jules Verne used
this information for his classic novel *Around the World
in Eighty Days*). Hence, a person who woke up on
Thursday could sail into Wednesday.

90   The third hand on a clock or a watch (not digi-
tal ones!) is called the second hand. Confusing, isn't
it?

91   Those are all names of horses that have won the
Kentucky Derby.

92 It wasn't raining.

93 This man was bald.

94. Absolutely false. Michelangelo painted his great works of art on the ceiling of the Sistine Chapel.

95 Christmas and New Year's Day always fall within the same twelve months.

96 A hailstone gets lighter (as it melts) the more you carry it around.

97 Cream is on the top of the milk, hence it is lighter than the milk.

98 Both weigh one pound.

99 Stand on a chair five feet off the floor. The egg can then fall three feet through the air without breaking. It won't break until it hits the floor.

100 The man who fell off the ladder had been standing on the bottom rung when he fell.

101 You might as well take the seven holes in your head, because that's what you have anyway (mouth, two eyes, two ear holes, two nostrils).

102 Yes, if you say *Washington, D.C.*

103 A pair of roller skates.

104 A leaf.

105 There were originally 27 potatoes on the platter.

106 There are ten children in the Harris family. Each daughter has two brothers, but they are the same two brothers.

107 Here are four 5's arranged so that they total 6:

$$\frac{55}{5} - 5 = 6$$

108 The fish weighs 20 pounds.

109 You have 60 cents in pennies, you have 39 dimes ($3.90), and you have one half-dollar.

110 You have a dime and a nickel. One of the coins is not a dime while the other, of course, is.

111   Yes, it is possible to have $63 in bills. You could have a fifty-dollar bill, plus a five-dollar bill, plus four two-dollar bills. You could also have one unpaid bill from the electric company for $63!

112   1,980 pennies equals $19.80, which is almost $20.

113   If you said 64, you answered too quickly. There are 204 squares in all—that is, if you take into consideration the 64 one-by-one squares, the 42 two-by-two squares, the 36 three-by-three squares, and so on.

114   First fill up the four-gallon pail. Take the four gallons and pour them into the seven-gallon pail. Refill the four-gallon pail and pour three gallons from that pail into the seven-gallon pail (since it already had four gallons in it, when it is filled to the top you know you have poured three more gallons into it). You now have one gallon left in the four-gallon pail. Completely empty the seven-gallon pail. Take the one gallon left in the four-gallon pail and pour it into the seven-gallon pail. Fill the four-gallon pail and pour that water into the seven-gallon pail. You now have five gallons of water in the seven-gallon pail.

115   There is no dirt in a hole 6 feet long, 8 feet deep, and 10 feet wide. If there were dirt in it, it would not be a hole.

116   One person takes the plate with the doughnut on it.

117   If the box was already filled with pears, she couldn't add any more pears to it.

118 You won't meet any buses at all if the buses travel by different routes. However, let us assume that the buses travel the same highways. When you leave Reno, there are already 10 buses on the road coming from Boston to Reno. During your trip, 10 more buses will leave Boston. So you should see 20 buses in all heading toward Reno.

119 The world would not increase in weight at all, since all the building materials for the wall would come from the earth itself.

120 To prove that half of 8 is 3, divide the number vertically. $8 = 3$

121 There are quite a few solutions to this problem. Here are five possible answers:

$123 + 4 - 5 + 67 - 89 = 100$ TRICKY SOLUTION:

$98\frac{3}{6} + 1\frac{27}{54} = 100$

$95\frac{3}{7} + 4\frac{16}{28} = 100$

$94\frac{1}{2} + 5\frac{38}{76} = 100$

```
    15
    36
    47
    98
   +2
   100
```

122   11
    1
    1
    1
  14

123 If you take five pennies from 100 pennies, you obviously have the five pennies that you take away.

124 Actually neither is correct—18 plus 19 is 37!

125 Most people will say that it takes two hours for the man to dig the hole, but, in fact, it will take the man twice as long as before to double the length, twice as long as before to double the width, and twice as long as before to double the hole's depth. So the correct answer is 2 × 2 × 2, or eight hours.

126 If you said that the pen cost one dollar, you answered too quickly. The pen cost $1.05. The bottle of ink cost a nickel.

127 The nine-digit number that satisfies the condition is: 219,438,657. ($219 \times 3 = 657$; $657 - 219 = 438$)

128 Hold the numbers up to a mirror. Nine plus one plus eight equals eighteen. (Would we lie to you?)

129 Here is one way to show that it is possible to subtract 45 from 45 and still get 45 for a total:

$$\begin{array}{r} 9+8+7+6+5+4+3+2+1=45 \\ -1+2+3+4+5+6+7+8+9=45 \\ \hline 8+6+4+1+9+7+5+3+2=45 \end{array}$$

130 You will have one big pile of leaves.

131 Choose the barrel of dimes, because more dimes will fit into the barrel. The barrel of dimes is worth (in face value) $96,536. The barrel of quarters is worth (in face value) $87,975.

132 To make the equation (560 = 600) correct, insert two sets of colons: 5:60 = 6:00 on a clock!

133 The person who buys the pawn ticket for three dollars loses on the transaction, because he or she will have to pay an additional four dollars to redeem the five-dollar bill from the pawnshop. The five-dollar bill, therefore, will cost that person seven dollars.

134   Take the second offer. If the month has 31 days, here is how much you would earn:

Day 1—1	Day 17—$655.36
Day 2—2	Day 18—$1,310.72
Day 3—4	Day 19—$2,621.44
Day 4—8	Day 20—$5,242.88
Day 5—.16	Day 21—$10,485.76
Day 6—.32	Day 22—$20,971.52
Day 7—.64	Day 23—$41,943.04
Day 8—1.28	Day 24—$83,886.08
Day 9—2.56	Day 25—$167,772.16
Day 10—5.12	Day 26—$335,544.32
Day 11—10.24	Day 27—$671,088.64
Day 12—20.48	Day 28—$1,342,177.28
Day 13—40.96	Day 29—$2,684,354.56
Day 14—81.92	Day 30—$5,368,709.12
Day 15—$163.84	Day 31—$10,737,418.24
Day 16—$327.68	

Thus, you would earn a total of $21,474,836.47.

135   The top and bottom numbers of dice always add up to seven. (You can use this information to perform a "mind-reading" feat for your friends.)

136   One possible solution:

```
  173        85
  +4        +92
 ----       ----
  177       177
```

137   Since all but 10 cows died, the man would have 10 cows left.

138   792 is the difference. Six dozen dozen is 864 ($6 \times 12 \times 12$); one half a dozen dozen is 72 ($\frac{1}{2} \times 12 \times 12$). Subtract 72 from 864 and you get 792.

139   You should have written 12, 102 (11,000 + 1,100 + 2).

140   To make the equation an equality, add a straight line to the second plus sign, changing it to a 4. Hence, the new equation reads:

$$11 + 1,141 = 1,152$$

141   One way to use four 9's to express 100 is: $99\frac{9}{9}$

142   Most people who answer this question quickly will say 55. Alas, 55 is not the correct answer. The correct answer is 175. ($80 \div \frac{1}{2} = 160$. $160 + 15 = 175$)

143   To answer this question correctly, you count 5,6,7,8,9,10.

144   All the months of the year have at least 28 days.

145   The man was playing golf. In golf the lowest score wins. Incidentally, in the card game of Hearts, the person with the lowest score also wins.

146   There are 12 seconds in a year: January 2nd, February 2nd, March 2nd, and so on.

147   The first woman takes one cube (an odd number), and the second woman takes eight sugar cubes. Now isn't it odd that a woman would put eight cubes of sugar into her tea?

148   Hawaii. Try this question on your friends. You will be surprised how few people will think of the correct answer.

149   Good Friday was the name of a horse running at Wolverhampton Race Track. On Tuesday afternoon, June 21, 1864, he fell on the first hurdle. If you get a chance to see *The Thirty-nine Steps*, you may want to listen carefully for this brain teaser.

150   She arrived in Paris, Kentucky, and not in Paris, France.

151   Boxing. In boxing the judges keep the score for each round, and the spectators do not know how the judges scored each round until the match is over.

152   There is no silver at all in German silver. German silver is actually an alloy of copper, nickel, and zinc.

153   Water weighs less as a solid than it does as a liquid. At zero degrees centigrade the density of ice is .9175, whereas at zero degrees centigrade the density of water is .9988. You can observe the truth of this fact when you place an ice cube in a glass of water and the ice cube floats.

154   Yes, if you stand back to back.

155   Rossini was born on February 29th of a leap year; thus he celebrated his birthday every four years. So he was forty-four years old on his eleventh birthday.

156   The nail would be at the very same place, since trees grow at their tops.

157   Yes, if the piece of paper is slid under a door. Slide a sheet of newspaper under a door, and have one person stand on the newspaper on one side of the door and the second person stand on the newspaper on the other side of the door.

158   How many states in the United States? You could say 50, and you probably did. But if you wish to be perfectly accurate, you should say that the United States consists of 45 states and five commonwealths.

Five states in the United States designate themselves as commonwealths: Maryland, Pennsylvania, Virginia, Kentucky, and Massachusetts. A commonwealth is a self-governing, autonomous political unit. Puerto Rico, not yet a state, is designated as a commonwealth.

159 There are no peas in a bushel of black-eyed peas. Black-eyed peas are really beans. Now please mind your *P*'s and *Q*'s or you'll be full of beans!

160 If you could count out a hundred dollars in one-dollar bills in 45 seconds, it would take you about 14 years and 98 days of constant counting to count one billion dollars.

161 All-metal shoes are worn by horses in the sport of horse-racing.

162 On a 33⅓-rpm long-playing record there is just one groove to each side. The groove starts from the outer edge and continues toward the center in one continuous winding.

163 The sloth. It hangs upside down in trees and swings from branch to branch.

164 Astounding as it may seem, this statement is true. You see, 1752 was the year that the great calendar reform took place. In that year September 2nd was designated September 14th. Hence, the dates

September 3rd through the 13th were stricken from the records of American history.

165 Badminton. Players use a shuttlecock (sometimes called a bird) in place of a ball.

166 India ink was first made in China, not in India at all.

167 The first day of the twenty-first century will be January 1, 2001. The first day of the twentieth century was January 1, 1901. (We toss in that information at no extra charge!)

168 Tug-of-war, rowing, and backstroke swimming.

169 A chain is a unit of measurement consisting of 100 links.

170 The man was living in Ceylon, where bamboo grows very tall. Bamboo, you see, is a type of grass.

171 True. A stack of one billion one-dollar bills would reach slightly over 69 miles high.

172 Arm, toe, eye, gum, jaw, hip, leg, lip, ear, and rib. You may wish to accept *gut* as an answer, too.

173 The derivative of saltpeter is called Mother of Saltpeter. Therefore, saltpeter is older than its mother.

174 Yes, in a legal sense. Suppose a widower and his son both marry. The father marries the daughter of a widow, and the man's son married the young woman's mother. The son would therefore become the father to his own father, and grandfather to his father's son—that is, himself.

175   The pitcher is brought in to pitch during the first half of the ninth inning with the score tied and with two outs. There is a runner on first base. The pitcher picks the runner off, thus retiring the side. His team comes to bat in the bottom of the ninth and scores the winning run.

176   The pitcher came in as a reliever in the first inning. The starting pitcher had given up two walks and a home run before the relief pitcher came in.

177   A   nickle   is   a   green-colored   woodpecker (you might want to look up the word in a good dictionary). The correct way to spell the coin is N-I-C-K-E-L.

178   Shakespeare's comedy *A Midsummer Night's Dream* does not take place in midsummer at all. The play, in fact, takes place between April 29th and May 1st (May Day). May Day is perhaps the most suitable wedding day for Hippolyta and Theseus.

179   An egg has to be broken before it is used; a horse has to be broken before it can be ridden.

180   True. Boiling the water drives out some of the air bubbles that slow down the freezing process.

181   You are actually sailing from north to south.

182   Gail, Mary, Sadie, Lena, and She were actually men who played, at one time or another, major-league baseball.

183   If you accept a fraction as an answer, you could say $\frac{1}{99}$. The smallest whole number that can be expressed with just three integers is 1, expressed by the following: 1$1^1$.

184 The ounce we have in mind is the snow leopard. The snow leopard, also called an ounce, weighs between 50 and 90 pounds.

185 If you turn that number upside down, it spells out the name—Illinois.

186 Alaska. Alaska's chain of islands stretch so far west that they actually cross the eastern meridian.

187 Night falls but does not break. Leaves fall but don't break. Day breaks but does not fall.

188 The first satellite to go around the earth was the moon. (Note that we didn't ask about "artificial" or "man-made" satellites.)

189   Their countries were using different calendars. England was using the Julian Calendar, Spain the Gregorian Calendar. There is a difference of ten days between the two calendars.

190   In theory, there could be a game with no official at-bats. The pitchers could walk all the batters and then pick the batters off first base.

191   The National Anthem of Hawaii is "The Star-Spangled Banner."

192   Would you believe 6009? Don't rush. You have plenty of time to get ready.

193   Gladys Godding, who was the organist at Ebbets Field.

194   Ten pitches. The batter could come to bat with two outs and with a runner on first base. The batter then takes five pitches so that the count goes to three and two. Then the runner is picked off first or is thrown out in an attempted steal. The batter then will come to bat in the next inning and could go to still another three and two count (three balls and two strikes) before making a hit, fouling a ball off, or drawing a walk.

195   If the man is *living* in New York City, why should he be buried at all?

196   If you said President Grant, you are only half right. President Grant's wife, Julia, is also buried there.

197   Probably a knapsack.

198 Footsteps.

199 Holes.

200 An anchor.

201 A piece of paper. If you toss it into the ocean, the paper will become so wet that it will break apart.

202 Milk can turn sour without moving. A child could turn eleven years old—or any other age—without moving.

203 Money goes further the slower it goes.

204 A person who gambles is a bettor, but a person who refuses to gamble is no bettor (better).

205 No, fish bite at worms.

206 The library.

207 A farmer who works day and night grows tired.

208 The best way to prevent water from coming into your house is not to pay the water bill.

209 A bald head.

210 An automobile grows less tired (its tires get worn down) the more it works.

211 Don't give it anything to eat.

212 The alarm clock.

213 Gossip.

214 A spoiled child is usually fresh.

215 The barber would prefer to shave 10 men from

anywhere because he or she earns more money that way.

216   Buy duck eggs.

217   Warm.

218   Income tax forms 1040 and 1040A.

219   Your reflection.

220   A duck's heart.

221   Windows in Detroit are glass.

222   Footprints.

223   The butcher weighs more—he weighs things all day long.

224   The best way to raise carrots is to pull them out by their tops.

225   The easiest thing for a hunter to catch in a heavy winter rain is a cold!

226 It depends on how many children are playing in the yard at the time.

227 Use a paperweight.

228 The milkman.

229 Hippopotamuses (hippopotami?) have baby hippopotamuses (or hippopotami).

230 All animals eat with their tails. At least, they don't remove their tails while eating.

231 His or her nose.

232 No candles burn longer. They all burn shorter.

233 His or her breath.

234 The doors and windows.

235 *Rust* eats iron but never swallows.

236 We never borrow thanks, but we often return it.

237 A spur.

238 A towel gets wetter and wetter the more it dries people's hands.

239 Reservations.

240 Noise.

241 An astronaut or a human cannonball has to be fired first.

242   A shoe.

243   Cracks.

244   Make the coat and vest first.

245   An ice-skating rink.

246   A pair of scissors.

247   One horse tail would do it, if the tail was long enough!

248   Heat is faster. Anyone can catch cold.

249   A bus or taxi driver.

250   A knife sharpener.

251   It gets wet.

252   None. (The other fly will fly away.)

253   O-hi-O.

254   Mustard.

255   Snow.

256   Your name.

257   Your word.

258   Your breath.

259   Carson City, Nevada, lies west of Los Angeles. Therefore, the man will have to drive east (or else he'll have to drive clear around the world!).

260   Yes, if the man happens to be a clergyman performing wedding ceremonies.

261   They can vote for the mayor of Boston.

262   Queen Elizabeth I was never married.

263   The Unfinished Symphony was started by Schubert, not Beethoven.